the Joy
Journal

"Hope is the thing with feathers
That perches in the soul,
And sings the tune without the words
And never stops at all."

Emily Dickinson

The Joy Journal

Published by The Humor Potential, Inc.
20 North Street #4, Plymouth, MA 02360

For book trade ordering contact:
The Humor Potential, Inc.
20 North Street #4, Plymouth, MA 02360
tel: 1-800-998-2324
E-mail: stressed@tiac.com
Web Site: www.stressed.com

Printed in the United States of America
by Bookcrafters, Chelsea, MI

ISBN: 0-9644014-7-9

Cover Illustration, Design and Layout by
ROBIN OUELLETTE, MIND'S EYE DESIGN

To all of those who wish for
more joy in their lives—
Here is the first step ....

Joy is an inner song that you sound as you move throughout the day. The most exciting thing we can do is to live joyfully. Joy comes from self acceptance, compassion for others and understanding that we are not the center of the universe. It expands within us, as we become acquainted with our purpose and follow our path. It lights up others when we love them for who they are, not what we wish they would become. When we are thankful for what we have, our joy soars, for gratitude is the mother of joy. It is our hope that you will write in your Joy Journal daily to express your delight in the gift of life.

As you write, reflect and savor what you have written, so that feelings of abundance can grow within you. Each week, review your joys and share some of them with family and friends. In other words, spread it around ... I hope you will, as "they" say, "EN<u>JOY</u>"!

For life is a buffet, with one exception, you don't get seconds .... so fill up your plate now!

TADAH !
from Loretta LaRoche

January

Meditation

"Our minds possess the power of healing pain and creating joy. If we use that power along with proper living, a positive attitude, and meditation, we can heal not only our mental and emotional afflictions, but even physical problems."

Tulku Thondup Rinpoche
a Buddhist scholar

A <u>Meditation</u> a Day
Keeps the Doctor Away

Pioneering research by Dr. Herbert Bensen and others has shown that meditation can have a profound impact on our lives. It not only slows down our brain waves, but can reduce stress and lower your blood pressure. If you've never practiced any meditation techniques before, it's simple enough to get started. The critical first step is that you just "do it!"

• Find 10 to 20 minutes in your daily routine that can be yours and yours alone. It's best if it's the same time every day, and for many, it's easiest in the morning.

• Find a quiet spot where you can sit in a comfortable chair, or better still, lie down.

• Do what you can to eliminate any predictable distractions in your household—(and yes, that includes your kids, the phone, the fax and the beeper) if necessary enlist the help of your spouse or loved one, but your ultimate objective is to demand some "quiet time."

• Now close your eyes, and begin to relax your muscles.

• If there are hundreds of thoughts buzzing through your mind, for the next few minutes, let them leave you. (They certainly aren't going anywhere, and you know they'll be there when you return.

• Now pick a word or short phrase that you can focus on—one that evokes a feeling of calm and serenity. Be sure to select a word that's easy to repeat, and one that doesn't elicit any negative memories or anxieties. ie. love, peace, happiness... whatever it is, pick what works for you.

• Begin breathing slowly and naturally and repeat your focus word silently as you exhale.

• If you prefer, you can also eliminate the use of a word and simply concentrate on the sound of your own breathing.

• If any ideas or thoughts ramble (creep) into your mind, simply say "oh well" and continue quietly breathing.

• When you feel ten or so peaceful minutes have "passed by" gently open your eyes.

• Don't jump up the minute that you're done.Remain quietly seated or lying down for another minute or two.

• Practice this exercise once or twice a day for the rest of your life!

• And please don't put it off till tomorrow. Give yourself a gift and begin today.

Dr. Herbert Bensen
"The Relaxation Response"

> "Meditation is simply about being yourself and knowing about who that is. It is about coming to realize that you are on a path, whether you like it or not, namely the path that is your life."
>
> Jon Kabat-Zinn

January 1 Happy New Year!

_____

_____

_____

_____

_____

_____

_____

_____

January 2

_____

_____

_____

_____

_____

_____

_____

_____

January 3

_____
_____
_____
_____
_____

January 4

_____
_____
_____
_____
_____

January 5

_____
_____
_____
_____
_____

January 6

_____
_____
_____
_____
_____

January 7

_____
_____
_____
_____
_____

January 8

_____
_____
_____
_____
_____

January 9

_____
_____
_____
_____
_____

January 10

_____
_____
_____
_____
_____

January 11

_____
_____
_____
_____
_____
_____
_____
_____
_____

January 12

_____
_____
_____
_____
_____
_____
_____
_____
_____

"Meditation is the art of paying attention. One way to develop your ability to give your undivided attention to what you are doing is to practice meditating. People often confuse meditation with withdrawing from the world, but it's actually a powerful technique for helping you to embrace the world more fully and enjoy your life more completely."

Dean Ornish, "Weigh Less, Eat More"

"Winter, a lingering season, is a time to gather golden moments, embark upon a sentimental journey, and enjoy every idle hour."

John Boswell

January 13

_____
_____
_____
_____
_____
_____
_____
_____

January 14

_____
_____
_____
_____
_____
_____
_____
_____

January 15

January 16

January 17

January 18

January 19

_____
_____
_____
_____
_____

January 20

_____
_____
_____
_____
_____

January 21

_____
_____
_____
_____
_____

January 22

_____
_____
_____
_____
_____

January 23

_____
_____
_____
_____
_____
_____
_____
_____
_____

January 24

_____
_____
_____
_____
_____
_____
_____
_____
_____

"To have a sacred place....is an absolute necessity for anybody today. You must have a room or a certain hour or so a day, where.... you can simply experience and bring forth what you are and what you might be."

Joseph Campbell
The Power and Myth

"Meditation is the key to the morning
and the latch of the evening."

Mohandas Gandhi

January 25

_____

_____

_____

_____

_____

January 26

_____

_____

_____

_____

_____

January 27

_____

_____

_____

_____

_____

_____

January 28

_____
_____
_____
_____

January 29

_____
_____
_____
_____

January 30

_____
_____
_____
_____

January 31 Put "Meditate" on your "to do" List!

_____
_____
_____
_____

February

Love and Spirituality

"Love has no other desire but to fulfill
itself, to melt and be like a running
brook that sings its melody to the
night, to wake at dawn with a winged
heart and give thanks for another
day of living."

Kahlil Gibran

Love is a feeling in the body, in the emotions and ultimately in the spiritual realms. Love overcomes obstacles to personal growth. It is seeing the larger picture of people's lives and focusing upon not what you want from them, but how you can assist them in their highest good.

Think for a moment of tomorrow. Are there things you could do to give love to someone or to experience more love yourself? Who in your life has given you unconditional love?

Take a few minutes to write a private
"thank you"....
Say what's in your heart.

Can you think of times when you were
so filled with love, you thought you
would burst ... Write it down.

"Spirituality is as much an ability to accept love as it is a capacity for loving, a constant two-way traffic into the heart."

Francis du Plessix Gray
author

February 1

_____
_____
_____
_____
_____
_____
_____
_____
_____

February 2

_____
_____
_____
_____
_____
_____
_____
_____
_____

February 3

February 4

February 5

February 6

February 7

_____
_____
_____
_____
_____

February 8

_____
_____
_____
_____
_____

February 9

_____
_____
_____
_____
_____

February 10

_____
_____
_____
_____
_____

February 11

_____
_____
_____
_____
_____
_____
_____
_____

February 12

_____
_____
_____
_____
_____
_____
_____
_____

"If you have just one person with whom you can
be weak, miserable, contrite and who won't hurt
you for it, then you are rich."

Margarete Buber-Neuman
Milena

"We are each of us angels with only one wing. And we can fly by embracing each other."

Luciano de Crescenzo

February 13

_____
_____
_____
_____
_____
_____
_____
_____
_____

February 14 Buy yourself chocolates!

_____
_____
_____
_____
_____
_____
_____
_____

February 15

_____
_____
_____
_____
_____

February 16

_____
_____
_____
_____
_____

February 17

_____
_____
_____
_____
_____

February 18

_____
_____
_____
_____
_____

February 19

February 20

February 21

February 22

February 23

_____
_____
_____
_____
_____
_____
_____
_____
_____

February 24

_____
_____
_____
_____
_____
_____
_____
_____
_____

" Love is like a violin. The music may stop now
and then, but the strings remain forever."

Bacher

"Love is like a beautiful flower which I may
not touch, but whose fragrance makes the
garden a place of delight just the same."

Helen Keller

February 25

_____

_____

_____

_____

_____

_____

_____

_____

February 26

_____

_____

_____

_____

_____

_____

_____

_____

_____

February 27

February 28

"Life is Paradise for those who love many
things with a passion."

Leo Buscaglia

March

Optimism/New Beginnings

"If you expect the worst and get the
worst you suffer twice.
If you expect the best and get the
worst, you only suffer once."

anonymous

Going From Oh No! to Ah Ha!
Tips for becoming more Optimistic

Happily Ever After:
- Criticize less
- Motivate your mate (no nagging allowed)
- Choose a common cause to donate your time to
- Catch your significant other doing something right
- Watch movies with positive role models
- Take ten minutes each to share good news
- Celebrate your love often

Parenting:
- Be consistent
- Set realistic goals
- Turn failures into a challenge
- Model optimistic behavior
- Make sure activities are age-appropriate
- Challenge your children's pessimistic views

Workplace:
- Keep your goals in mind
- Hang out with upbeat people
- Pay attention to your health
- Become a creative problem-solver,
  not a problem-maker
- Realize you have options,
  you don't have to die at your desk
- Greet your co-workers with a cheerful comment

Stress:
- Don't catastrophize and awfulize
- STOP "mind-reading"
- Practice letting go
- Find the bless in the mess
- Remember, "This too shall pass"

Enhancing You

Every morning when you wake up, you are literally being given the opportunity to redirect your life. As you get up shout, "I'm Back!" Once you have evaluated past mistakes, let them go, and focus on what you are going to create today.

Open your heart and mind to the excitement of possibilities. Smile often and open the door to new friendships. Renew what you have lost in your self: enthusiasm, spontaneity, a childlike wonder for a pile of leaves, a puddle, a funny little bug. Expand the unique you, have fun with yourself as if you were the most interesting person to be with.

Being open to accept new things, ideas, and people into your life creates an ever expanding capacity for joy.

Loretta LaRoche

"Only one person in this world can ever make you feel depressed, worried or angry - and that person is you! This idea can change your life."

David Burns
Ten Days to Self-Esteem

March 1

_____
_____
_____
_____
_____
_____
_____
_____
_____

March 2

_____
_____
_____
_____
_____
_____
_____
_____
_____
_____

March 3

_____
_____
_____
_____
_____

March 4

_____
_____
_____
_____
_____

March 5

_____
_____
_____
_____
_____

March 6

_____
_____
_____
_____
_____

March 7

March 8

March 9

My father died tonight, at 11:15 P.M.

March 10

March 11

March 12

"Worry is a futile thing, it's
somewhat like a rocking chair.
Although it keeps you occupied,
it doesn't get you anywhere."

unknown

"Optimists may live longer...Pessimists may be accurate but they don't live as long."

anonymous

"If you think you can, you can. And if you think you can't, you're right."

Mary Kay Ash

March 13

March 14

March 15

_____
_____
_____
_____

March 16

_____
_____
_____
_____

March 17

_____
_____
_____
_____

March 18

_____
_____
_____
_____
_____

March 19

March 20 First Day of Spring!

March 21

March 22

March 23

_____
_____
_____
_____
_____
_____
_____
_____

March 24

_____
_____
_____
_____
_____
_____
_____
_____

"For Yesterday is but a Dream, and Tomorrow is
only a Vision; but Today, well-lived, makes every
Yesterday a Dream of Happiness, and every
Tomorrow a Vision of Hope."

unknown

"The Optimist proclaims that we live in the best of all possible worlds and the Pessimist fears this is true."

James Branch Cabell

March 25

_____
_____
_____
_____
_____
_____

March 26

_____
_____
_____
_____
_____
_____

March 27

_____
_____
_____
_____
_____
_____

March 28

_____
_____
_____
_____

March 29

_____
_____
_____
_____

March 30

_____
_____
_____
_____

March 31

_____
_____
_____
_____

April

Humor and Play

"If your whole world is upside down,
and joy and cheer are far from you,
romp for an hour with a six year old
child, and see if his laughter and
faith are not veritable sign-posts on
the road to happiness."

Gladys Harvey-Knight

From Misery to Mirth!

Tools and techniques to keep a light-hearted spirit!

Happily Ever Laughter:

How to relate with your mate with joy

- Hug a lot
- Have a party for two
- Say "Thank You" more often
- Put some funny jokes in each others pockets
- Watch funny movies together
- Wear a funny costume at dinner
- Make sure positive information outweighs
  the negative
- Decide which sit-com your relationship
  resembles in order to see the humor
  in each other

Parenting with Humor:

- Be flexible
- Celebrate for no reason at all
- Make play a priority
- Have a family "Humor Night"
- Use appropriate humor
  (not making fun of others)
- Start the day by sharing good news

Humor in the Workplace:

- The copier is not the enemy
- Give yourself a funny title
  (like The Grand Pubah of Everything)
- Have a staff laff
- Send a funny memo once in a while
- Don't whine with co-workers
- Keep a "Done" list on your desk

Humor Your Stress:

- Keep in mind that STRESSED spelled backwards is DESSERTS
- Don't wish for Friday if it's still Monday
- Keep a mirror handy, look at yourself, and periodically ask, "How Serious Is This?"
- Don't get caught up in judging everything and everybody, it's exhausting
- Wake up and put a smile on your face, your day will be more optimistic

---

Smiling from Inside Out

1. When you wake up, put a smile on your face and announce, "I'm Back!"

2. Spend time with children. Four year olds in particular, supposedly they laugh at least four hundred times a day.

3. Increase your smile connections. Smile at more people during the day...it will come back to you.

4. Consider spending part of each day smiling about what you have instead of what you need.

5. When you smile at someone, look into their eyes... it is the gateway to their soul.

Loretta LaRoche
excerpt from "How Serious Is This?"

"A person without a sense of humor is like a wagon without springs - jolted by every pebble in the road."

Henry Ward Beecher
19th Century American Clergyman

April 1 April Fool's Day - Wear a funny hat!

_____

_____

_____

_____

_____

_____

_____

_____

April 2

_____

_____

_____

_____

_____

_____

_____

_____

_____

April 3

_____
_____
_____
_____

April 4

_____
_____
_____
_____

April 5

_____
_____
_____
_____

April 6

_____
_____
_____
_____
_____

April 7

_____
_____
_____
_____
_____

April 8

_____
_____
_____
_____
_____

April 9

_____
_____
_____
_____
_____

April 10

_____
_____
_____
_____
_____

April 11

_____
_____
_____
_____
_____
_____
_____
_____
_____

April 12

_____
_____
_____
_____
_____
_____
_____
_____
_____

 "Humor does put you in a good mood... Usually when people are sick, or have something wrong, they get depressed. They can't do this, they can't do that... But if you start to laugh, it'll change your mood. It's a feeling of 'I Can', instead of 'I Can't'. Because depression is 'I Can't', and laughing is 'I Can'."

Sid Caesar

"Cheerfulness and contentment are great beautifiers, and are famous preservers of good looks."

Charles Dickens

"From there to here to there, funny things are everywhere!"

Dr. Seuss

April 13

_____
_____
_____
_____
_____
_____
_____
_____
_____

April 14

_____
_____
_____
_____
_____
_____
_____
_____
_____
_____

April 15

_____
_____
_____
_____

April 16

_____
_____
_____
_____

April 17

_____
_____
_____
_____

April 18

_____
_____
_____
_____

April 19

_____
_____
_____
_____

April 20

_____
_____
_____
_____

April 21

_____
_____
_____
_____

April 22

_____
_____
_____
_____

April 23

April 24

"Humor is one of the truly elegant defenses in
the human repertoire. Few would deny that the
capacity for humor, like hope, is one of
mankind's most important antidotes for the
woes of Pandora's Box"

George Valiiant
Adaptation to Life

> "You can't really be strong until you see a funny side of things."
>
> Ken Kesey

April 25

April 26

April 27

April 28

_____

_____

_____

_____

_____

April 29

_____

_____

_____

_____

_____

April 30

_____

_____

_____

_____

_____

"Pointing out the comic elements of a situation can bring a sense of proportion and perspective to what might otherwise seem an overwhelming problem."

Harvey Mindness

May

Health and Nutrition

"The first wealth is health."
Ralph Waldo Emerson

"There are no riches above a
sound body, and no joy above
the joy of the heart."

anonymous

From "Healthy Pleasures"
by Robert Ornstein, Ph.D.
and David Sobel. M.D.

Our physiology does not stop at our skin, nor does our health. Consider the heart; feelings of hostility and isolation of oneself from others appear to damage the heart. Self centered people who feel apart from others, not a part of a larger social body, are more likely to succumb to heart disease. Disruptions of relationships with other people can profoundly disrupt health, which accounts for the spikes of illness after the loss of a loved one or after moving to a new city or country.

Men and women form social relationships, whether to spouses, friends, companies, societies, or even pets. In ancient times these social groups enhanced health in many practical ways; bringing up offspring, hunting and gathering, and cooperating against predators. Our connection to others is still vital. The idea of survival is not just about the individual, but about the species ...

Health Facts and Advice:

Fact: According to John Bradshaw. "Addiction to worry takes a tremendous toll on the body because it forces us to live in a constant state of alertness, prepared to fight or run."

Advice: One Technique Bradshaw uses is replacing insecure thoughts with secure thoughts, ie. What is the best thing that could happen from this experience?

Fact: A hostile, cynical outlook on life doesn't just foster bad feelings: It's also linked to an increased risk of heart disease.

Advice: Cool your anger: Exercising 20-40 minutes a day, 4 or 5 times a week is a good way to dispel frustration and anxiety. Meditation and biofeedback can also lower your blood pressure and stress hormone levels.

Fact: A University of Michigan survey showed that doing regular volunteer work, more than any other activity, dramatically increased life expectancy (and probably vitality).

Advice: Adopt a new definition of health. One that involves other people and not just the individual. You may live longer!

Fact: Six percent of all people experience an acute form of SAD, Season Affective Disorder. It is caused by light deprivation and it's onset can be triggered by factors such as stress.

Advice: There is relief. According to scientist Robert Levin, Ph.D., people with SAD who light a few cool white florescent bulbs while working, reading, or watching TV, cheer up. (Lears, 1991)

"If women were convinced that a day or an hour of solitude was a reasonable ambition, they would find a way of attaining it. As it is, they feel so unjustified in their demand that they rarely make the attempt."

Anne Morrow Lindbergh

May 1

_____
_____
_____
_____
_____
_____
_____
_____
_____

May 2

_____
_____
_____
_____
_____
_____
_____
_____
_____
_____

May 3

May 4

May 5

May 6

May 7

May 8

May 9

May 10

May 11

_____
_____
_____
_____
_____
_____
_____
_____
_____

May 12

_____
_____
_____
_____
_____
_____
_____
_____
_____

"The Art of medicine consists of keeping the patient amused while nature heals the disease."

Voltaire

"You only live once—But if you work it out right, once is enough."

Joe E. Lewis

May 13

_____

_____

_____

_____

_____

_____

_____

_____

May 14

_____

_____

_____

_____

_____

_____

_____

_____

_____

May 15

_____
_____
_____
_____
_____

May 16

_____
_____
_____
_____
_____

May 17

_____
_____
_____
_____
_____

May 18

_____
_____
_____
_____
_____

May 19

_____

_____

_____

_____

_____

May 20

_____

_____

_____

_____

_____

May 21

_____

_____

_____

_____

_____

May 22

_____

_____

_____

_____

_____

May 23

_____
_____
_____
_____
_____
_____
_____
_____
_____

May 24

_____
_____
_____
_____
_____
_____
_____
_____
_____

"It pays to be happy. Happiness is not a luxury, but a necessity. The beneficial effect of mental sunshine on life, ability, strength, vitality, endurance, is most pronounced."

Christina D. Larson

"Blessed is the one who is too busy to worry in the daytime and too sleepy to worry at night."

unknown

May 25

_____

_____

_____

_____

_____

_____

May 26

_____

_____

_____

_____

_____

_____

May 27

_____

_____

_____

_____

_____

_____

May 28

_____
_____
_____
_____

May 29

_____
_____
_____
_____

May 30

_____
_____
_____
_____

May 31

_____
_____
_____
_____

June

Music, Art, Dance

"I have heard of the rainbows, of the stars, of the play of light upon the waves. These I would like to see. But far more than sight, I wish for my ears to be opened. The voice of a friend, the happy busy noises of community, the imaginations of Mozart. Life without these is darker by far than blindness."

Helen Keller

The Best Things In Life Are Free

(From "Good News")

Words and Music by B.G. DeSylva, Lew Brown and Ray Henderson

The   moon   be - longs   to

ev - 'ry - one,_____   The   Best Things In   Life   Are

Free, _____   The   stars   be - long   to

ev - 'ry - one _____   They gleam there for you   and

me. _____ The flow-ers in Spring,__ The

rob-ins that sing,____ The sun-beams that shine____They're

your's, They're mine! And love can come to

ev-'ry - one,_____ The Best Things In Life Are Free.

"Develop interest in life as you see it in people, things, literature, music—The world is so rich, simply throbbing with rich treasures, beautiful souls and interesting people. Forget yourself."

Henry Miller

June 1

_____
_____
_____
_____
_____
_____
_____
_____

June 2

_____
_____
_____
_____
_____
_____
_____
_____
_____

June 3

_____
_____
_____
_____

June 4

_____
_____
_____
_____

June 5

_____
_____
_____
_____

June 6

_____
_____
_____
_____
_____

June 7

_____
_____
_____
_____

June 8

_____
_____
_____
_____

June 9

_____
_____
_____
_____

June 10

_____
_____
_____
_____

June 11

_____
_____
_____
_____
_____
_____
_____
_____
_____

June 12

_____
_____
_____
_____
_____
_____
_____
_____

"I think I should have no other mortal wants, if I could always have plenty of music. It seems to infuse strength into my limbs and ideas into my brain. Life seems to go on without effort, when I am filled with music."

George Elliot

"I celebrate myself, and sing myself."
Walt Whitman
Song of Myself

June 13

June 14

June 15

_____
_____
_____
_____
_____

June 16

_____
_____
_____
_____
_____

June 17

_____
_____
_____
_____
_____

June 18

_____
_____
_____
_____
_____

June 19

June 20

June 21 First Day of Summer

June 22

June 23

_____
_____
_____
_____
_____
_____
_____
_____
_____

June 24

_____
_____
_____
_____
_____
_____
_____
_____
_____

"Look at kid's drawings.... having the sun with rays coming off it to try and represent the warmth that you feel from the sun ... kids actually play out their understanding of the world in the drawings they do."

Rob Semper

"The brook would lose its song if
you removed its rocks."
unknown

June 25

_____
_____
_____
_____
_____
_____

June 26

_____
_____
_____
_____
_____
_____

June 27

_____
_____
_____
_____
_____
_____
_____

June 28

June 29

June 30

"Fine art is that in which the hand, the head,
and the heart of man go together."

John Ruskin

July
Journeys/Nature

"This curious world which we inhibit is more wonderful than it is convenient, more beautiful than it is useful; it is more to be admired and enjoyed than used."

Henry David Thoreau

The Journey to Joy

1. Practice Kindness
   Catch someone doing something right

2. Live with Passion
   I Love You!, It's Delicious!

3. Savor feelings of abundance
   Keep a Joy Journal

4. Keep wonder and surprise
   in your daily life;
   Prevents cynicism

5. Forgive and let go
   Keeps you feeling lighter

6. Express yourself
   Karate Yell, Paint, Sing, Dance

7. Celebrate as often as possible
   Menopause Party, Flu Season Party

8. Inspire yourself -
   Give yourself an alter ego
   The Prince of Pride, The Duchess of
   Doing, The Goddess of Guffaws

Let's Sing the Song of Life and be Grateful for all we love!

Loretta LaRoche
"Humor Your Stress"
PBS August, 1996

To Risk

To <u>Laugh</u> is to risk appearing the fool

To <u>Weep</u> is to risk appearing sentimental

To <u>Reach Out</u> to another is to risk involvement

To <u>Express Feelings</u> is to risk exposing your true self

To place <u>Ideas and Dreams</u> before a crowd

is to risk their loss

To <u>Love</u> is to risk loving in return

To <u>Live</u> is to risk dying

To <u>Hope</u> is to risk despair

To <u>Try</u> is to risk failure

But risks must be taken because the greatest hazard in life is to risk nothing. The person who asks nothing, does nothing, has nothing, and is nothing. They may avoid suffering and sorrow, but they cannot learn, feel, change, grow. love, live. Chained by their attitudes, they are a slave. They have forfeited their freedom.

Only a person who risks is free.

Anonymous

"A tree as great as a man's embrace
springs from a small shoot.
A terrace nine stories high
begins with a pile of earth.
A journey of a thousand miles
starts with the first step."

Lao-Tsu
Tao Te Ching

July 1

_____
_____
_____
_____
_____
_____
_____
_____

July 2

_____
_____
_____
_____
_____
_____
_____
_____

July 3

_____
_____
_____
_____
_____

July 4

_____
_____
_____
_____
_____

July 5

_____
_____
_____
_____
_____

July 6

_____
_____
_____
_____
_____

July 7

_____
_____
_____
_____
_____

July 8

_____
_____
_____
_____
_____

July 9

_____
_____
_____
_____
_____

July 10

_____
_____
_____
_____
_____

July 11

_____

_____

_____

_____

_____

_____

_____

_____

_____

July 12

_____

_____

_____

_____

_____

_____

_____

_____

_____

"The journey to self-discovery is the highest
adventure on earth and gives us an expanded
vision of what it means to be human."

Arianna Strassinopoulos
author

"Though we travel the world over to find the beautiful, we must carry it within us, or we find it not."

Ralph Waldo Emerson

July 13

July 14

July 15

July 16

July 17

July 18

July 19

_____
_____
_____
_____
_____

July 20

_____
_____
_____
_____
_____

July 21

_____
_____
_____
_____
_____

July 22

_____
_____
_____
_____
_____

July 23

_____
_____
_____
_____
_____
_____
_____
_____
_____

July 24

_____
_____
_____
_____
_____
_____
_____
_____
_____

"Nature speaks in symbols and signs."
John Greenleaf Whittier

"It is better to travel
hopefully than to arrive."
Japanese Proverb

July 25

_____
_____
_____
_____
_____
_____

July 26

_____
_____
_____
_____
_____
_____

July 27

_____
_____
_____
_____
_____
_____

July 28

_____
_____
_____
_____
_____

July 29

_____
_____
_____
_____
_____

July 30

_____
_____
_____
_____
_____

July 31

_____
_____
_____
_____
_____

August

Lighten Up
Your Stress

"Live each day as if it were
the last day of your life:
someday you will be right."

anonymous

Stressed? Let's Face It!

I firmly believe that a lot of stress can be handled with a big dose of common sense, lots of humor and a better grip on reality. We take life's little glitches and treat them as if they were as important as losing a job or as dangerous as being trapped in an avalanche. True, there are situations that are inconvenient, irritating or depressing, but a rational mind learns to discern the difference.

Too much "catastrophizing and awfulizing" can help trigger a response called "fight or flight". Walter B. Cannon, a physiologist at Harvard at the turn of the century, was the first to describe the "fight or flight" response as a series of biochemical changes that prepare you to deal with threats. Primitive man needed quick bursts of energy to flee such predators as the Saber-toothed Tiger.

However, if you're in your car in a traffic jam and you're yelling at people who can't even hear you, you're mobilizing a response that is no longer useful. Since the body doesn't know whether it's in a cave or a car, it responds to what it thinks are your cries for help. Your pupils dilate to sharpen vision and your hearing becomes acute. Your heart rate, blood volume, and blood pressure go up. You start to perspire. Your hands and feet get cold, as blood is directed away from your extremities and digestive system into larger muscles that help you to fight or run. Your diaphragm and anus lock. (this could be where the real meaning of uptight comes from!) You reach for a spear. In front of you is a seventy-eight year old woman in a thirty-eight year old Buick. She's enjoying her day because she knows moments are precious. She doesn't realize that in back of her is a raving Neanderthal who perceives her to be a Behemoth!

How many times a day do you get ready to throw the spear? The threats can be real or imagined and can run the gamut from dealing with a Xerox machine that won't work, to a long line at the checkout counter; from a bad haircut to a misbehaving toddler. Virtually anything can trigger the response if you think or interpret the situation as harmful or threatening. Chronic "fight or flight" can seriously harm you both physically and emotionally. The bad news being that every body system can be damaged by stress. The good news is that we all have the ability to change our way of viewing life's events. We may not be able to change the situation, but we can see it differently.

The use of humor can be one of the greatest resources we have in helping us restore our perspective when we've become "hooked on catastrophizing". Dr. William Fry Jr., who has done extensive research documenting the physiological benefits of laughter, notes that fear and rage, two emotions associated with stress, are countered and alleviated by humor. "Humor acts to relieve fear", he states, "rage is impossible when mirth prevails".

Loretta LaRoche
"How Serious Is This?"

"Hate, bitterness and vindictiveness
are overpowering, self-defeating and
intellectually as well as emotionally
depleting."

Dr. Gerald Jampolsky
Love is Letting Go of Fear

August 1

_____
_____
_____
_____
_____
_____
_____
_____
_____

August 2

_____
_____
_____
_____
_____
_____
_____
_____
_____

August 3

_____

_____

_____

_____

_____

August 4

_____

_____

_____

_____

_____

August 5

_____

_____

_____

_____

_____

August 6

_____

_____

_____

_____

_____

August 7

_____
_____
_____
_____
_____

August 8

_____
_____
_____
_____
_____

August 9

_____
_____
_____
_____
_____

August 10

_____
_____
_____
_____
_____

August 11

_____
_____
_____
_____
_____
_____
_____
_____
_____

August 12

_____
_____
_____
_____
_____
_____
_____
_____
_____

"We are what we think. All that we are
arises with our thoughts. With our
thoughts we create the world."

Buddha

"Forgiveness is letting what was, be gone;
what will be, come; and what is now, be."
David Augsburger

August 13

_____

_____

_____

_____

_____

_____

_____

_____

August 14

_____

_____

_____

_____

_____

_____

_____

_____

_____

August 15

August 16

August 17

August 18

August 19

August 20

August 21

August 22

August 23

August 24

"Anger is just one letter short of danger."

unknown

"We either make ourselves miserable, or
we make ourselves strong. The amount of
work is the same."

Carlos Castaneda
"Journey to Ixtlan"

"There is a beautiful and an ugly way in which to say almost everything, and happiness depends upon which way we take."

Delia L. Porter

August 25

_____
_____
_____
_____
_____
_____

August 26

_____
_____
_____
_____
_____
_____

August 27

_____
_____
_____
_____
_____
_____

August 28

_____
_____
_____
_____
_____

August 29

_____
_____
_____
_____
_____

August 30

_____
_____
_____
_____
_____

August 31

_____
_____
_____
_____
_____

September

Creativity

"Learn the craft of knowing
how to open your heart and
to turn on your creativity.
There's a light inside of you."

Judith Jamison

50 Ways to Get
Your Creative Juices Flowing

1. Eat dessert first
2. Spend the day with a five year old
3. Wear two different colored socks
4. Drive to work a different way
5. Study a subject you have no interest in
6. Take tap dancing lessons
7. Learn a new language
8. Spend ten minutes each day solving a problem
9. Go to the beach in January
10. Get up early and watch the sun rise
11. Say Thank you when someone criticizes you
12. Bake a cake without a recipe
13. Yell Hurrah in the bathroom
14. Go on a trip without planning it
15. Do something no one expects of you
16. Say hello to everyone you pass
17. Think of twenty different ways to use your bath tub
18. Record all your dreams for a week
19. Invite two people you don't like at work out to lunch
20. One day a week don't say anything negative
21. Make a list of things you don't have to do
22. Watch nothing but funny movies all day long
23. Have Thanksgiving twice
24. Stand in your yard and howl at the moon
25. Go to clown school
26. Make a collage of all the things you want to do with your life
27. Put a suggestion box in your home
28. Spend time brainstorming with co-workers on how to boost morale
29. Be in the moment as often as possible

30. Each day find out about something you know nothing about
31. Listen to what people say
32. Don't say I can't
33. Find out what's funny about yourself and tell everyone
34. Act enthusiastically about other peoples ideas
35. Send Christmas and Hanakuh cards in July
36. Put a rubber duck in your kids' lunch box
37. Put an ad in the newspaper about your birthday
38. Think of fifty ways you can be of service to the human race
39. Keep a journal of ideas
40. Daydream a few minutes every day
41. Don't criticize anyone one day a week
42. Give encouragement where it's needed
43. Write down one hundred ways you can use your talents
44. Record yourself for one day, how do you sound?
45. Wear a silly hat the next time you go shopping
46. Give yourself a ridiculous title and print it on business cards
47. Drive calmly through traffic
48. Look for something new in everything you do
49. Laugh out loud in a parking lot
50. Draw a picture of yourself being happy, frame it and hang it up!

by Loretta LaRoche

"If you do not express your own original ideas, if you do not listen to your being, you will have betrayed yourself."

Rollo May

September 1

_____
_____
_____
_____
_____
_____
_____
_____

September 2

_____
_____
_____
_____
_____
_____
_____
_____
_____

September 3

September 4

September 5

September 6

September 7

_____
_____
_____
_____
_____

September 8

_____
_____
_____
_____
_____

September 9

_____
_____
_____
_____
_____

September 10

_____
_____
_____
_____
_____

September 11

_____

_____

_____

_____

_____

_____

_____

_____

September 12

_____

_____

_____

_____

_____

_____

_____

_____

"Life is a great big canvas, and you should splash
all the paint on it you can!"

Carole Rae
Artist

"Inspiration lies at the intersection
of bold action and quiet reflection."
unknown

September 13

_____

_____

_____

_____

_____

_____

_____

_____

September 14

_____

_____

_____

_____

_____

_____

_____

_____

_____

September 15

_____
_____
_____
_____
_____

September 16

_____
_____
_____
_____
_____

September 17

_____
_____
_____
_____
_____

September 18

_____
_____
_____
_____
_____

September 19 Loretta's Birthday. Send Cards!

_____
_____
_____
_____
_____

September 20

_____
_____
_____
_____
_____

September 21

_____
_____
_____
_____
_____

September 22 First Day of Autumn

_____
_____
_____
_____
_____

September 23

September 24

"The man who makes no mistakes does not usually make anything."

Edward John Phelps
1899

"Let me listen to me and not to them."
Gertrude Stein

September 25

_____
_____
_____
_____
_____
_____

September 26

_____
_____
_____
_____
_____
_____

September 27

_____
_____
_____
_____
_____
_____
_____

September 28

September 29

September 30

"Fear is a perceived lack of options.
Creativity gives you options."
Roger Firestien

October

Imagination/Curiosity

"I suppose the moments one most enjoys are moments alone— when one unexpectedly stretches something inside that needs stretching."

Georgia O'Keefe

Imagination
by Patch Adams, M.D.
Author of "Gesundheit"

Everything comes from the imagination: its sacred graces can make life sparkle and make a person young at heart.

Everybody can stimulate imagination: it exists in every person. Like the physical body, imagination can become flabby if it is not exercised and appreciated. Here are some qualities that exercise the imagination:

- A glorious sense of wonder through contemplation and study of nature, humanity, the arts, and life itself.

- Exploration of all areas of interest, however briefly, and saying yes to every opportunity

- Sharing of ideas with every available person and studying ideas very different from one's own

- Enormous sense of play and improvisation, huge quantities of goal-free experimentation

- Tinkering in every artistic medium

- Restructuring one's life toward happiness

10 Ways to be
a Human Being—
Not a Human Doing!

- be silly
- be giving
- be playful
- be flexible
- be grateful
- be cheerful
- be optimistic
- be enthusiastic
- be willing to learn
- be available to loved ones

"You can't depend on your judgement
when your imagination is out of focus."
Mark Twain

October 1

_____
_____
_____
_____
_____
_____
_____
_____
_____

October 2

_____
_____
_____
_____
_____
_____
_____
_____
_____

October 3

October 4

October 5

October 6

October 7

_____

_____

_____

_____

_____

October 8

_____

_____

_____

_____

_____

October 9

_____

_____

_____

_____

_____

October 10

_____

_____

_____

_____

_____

October 11

October 12

"We are all of us imaginative in some form or
other, for images are the brood of desire."
George Elliot

"Imagination is not a talent of some men, but is the health of every man,"

Ralph Waldo Emerson

October 13

October 14

October 15

October 16

October 17

October 18

October 19

October 20

October 21

October 22

October 23

October 24

"The search is what anyone would
undertake if he were not sunk in the
everydayness of his own life. To become
aware of the possibility of the search
is to be on to something. Not to be on
to something is to be in despair."

Walker Percy

> "Life and love are life and love, a bunch of violets is a bunch of violets and to drag in the idea of a point is to ruin everything. Live and let live, love and let love, flower and fade, and follow the natural curve, which flows on pointless."
>
> D.H. Lawrence

October 25

_____
_____
_____
_____
_____
_____

October 26

_____
_____
_____
_____
_____
_____

October 27

_____
_____
_____
_____
_____
_____

October 28

_____
_____
_____
_____

October 29

_____
_____
_____
_____

October 30

_____
_____
_____
_____

October 31

_____
_____
_____
_____

November

Gratitude

"Gratitude unlocks the fullness of life. It turns what we have into enough and more. It turns denial into acceptance, chaos into order, confusion into clarity. It can turn a meal into a feast, a house into a home, a stranger into a friend. Gratitude makes sense of our past, brings peace for today, and creates a vision for tomorrow."

Melody Beattie

Prayers of Gratitude and Love

Lord, make me an instrument of your peace.
Where there is hatred, let me sow love.
Where there is injury, pardon.
Where there is doubt, faith.
Where there is despair, hope.
Where there is darkness, light.
And where there is sadness, joy.

O' Divine Master,
grant that I may not so much seek
to be consoled, as to console;
to be understood, as to understand;
to be loved, as to love.
For it is in giving that we receive—
It is in pardoning, that we are pardoned.
And it is in dying, that we are born to eternal life.

St. Francis of Assisi

Thank you God for having returned
my soul to my body today in your compassion.

Barrichot
Jewish Prayer

Ten thousand flowers in spring, the moon in autumn,
a cool breeze in summer, snow in winter,
If your mind isn't clouded by unnecessary things,
this is the best season of your life.

Wu-Men

What actions are most excellent?
To gladden the heart of a human being.
To feed the hungry. To help the afflicted.
To lighten the sorrow of the sorrowful.
To remove the wrongs of the injured.
That person is the most beloved of God—
who does most good to God's creations.

The Prophet Muhammad

The thought manifests as the word;
the word manifests as the deed;
the deed develops in habit;
and habit hardens into character.
So watch the thought and its ways with care,
and let it spring from love
born out of concern for all beings.

The Buddha

Make us worthy, Lord,
to serve others throughout the world
who live and die in poverty or hunger.
Give them, through our hands,
this day their daily bread
and by our understanding love,
give peace and joy.

Mother Theresa

"I would maintain that thanks are the highest form of thought, and that gratitude is happiness doubled by wonder."

GK Chesterton

November 1

_____
_____
_____
_____
_____
_____
_____
_____

November 2

_____
_____
_____
_____
_____
_____
_____
_____
_____

November 3

_____
_____
_____
_____
_____

November 4

_____
_____
_____
_____
_____

November 5

_____
_____
_____
_____
_____

November 6

_____
_____
_____
_____
_____

November 7

November 8

November 9

November 10

November 11

_____
_____
_____
_____
_____
_____
_____
_____
_____
_____

November 12

_____
_____
_____
_____
_____
_____
_____
_____
_____
_____

"Gratitude takes three forms; A feeling in
the heart, an expression in words, and giving
in return."

unknown

"Gratitude is the memory of the heart."

JB Massieu

November 13

_____
_____
_____
_____
_____
_____
_____
_____
_____

November 14

_____
_____
_____
_____
_____
_____
_____
_____
_____

November 15

November 16

November 17

November 18

November 19

_____
_____
_____
_____
_____

November 20

_____
_____
_____
_____
_____

November 21

_____
_____
_____
_____
_____

November 22

_____
_____
_____
_____
_____

November 23

November 24

"One can never pay in gratitude; one can only
pay "in kind" somewhere else in life."

Anne Morrow Lindbergh

> "When we say "Thank You",
> we've said it all."
> Loretta LaRoche

November 25

_____
_____
_____
_____
_____

November 26

_____
_____
_____
_____
_____

November 27

_____
_____
_____
_____
_____

November 28

_____
_____
_____
_____
_____

November 29

_____
_____
_____
_____
_____

November 30

_____
_____
_____
_____
_____

"Everything is holy! Everybody is holy!
Everywhere is holy! Everyday is an eternity!
Every man's an angel!"

Allen Ginsberg

December

The Gift of Giving

"When we share, that is
poetry in the prose of life."
Sigmund Freud

I know nothing else but miracles,
Whether I walk the streets of Manhattan,
Or dart my sight over the
roofs of houses toward the sky,
Or wade with naked feet along the beach
just in the edge of the water,
Or stand under trees in the woods,
Or talk by day with anyone I love,
Or sleep in bed at night with anyone I love,
Or sit at the table at dinner with the rest,
Or look at strangers opposite me riding in the car,
Or watch honey-bees busy around
the hive of a summer forenoon,
Or animals feeding in the fields,
Or birds, or the wonderfulness of insects in the air,
Or the exquisite delicate thin curve
of the new moon in the spring.
These with the rest, one and all, are to me miracles.
The whole referring, yet each distinct and in its place.
To me every hour of the light and dark is a miracle.
Every cubic inch of space is a miracle,
Every square yard of the surface
of the earth is spread with miracles.
Every foot of the interior swarms with miracles.

Walt Whitman

Gift Ideas From the
Heart and Soul

1. Home-made bread
2. Hug coupons
3. A meditation tape
4. A bag of penny candy
5. A massage
6. Assorted herbal teas
7. A yoga or Tai Chi class
8. Cook dinner for someone who can't get out
9. Volunteer to babysit for a young family
10. Photo of yourself as a baby
11. Take your family to an art museum
12. An " audio letter " for someone you love
13. A week of forgiveness
14. A coloring book and crayons to an adult
15. A video of yourself laughing

"To have a real life, people must participate in real community. People who live in virtual communities have virtual lives."

Mary Piper, Ph.D.
The Shelter of Each Other

December 1

_____
_____
_____
_____
_____
_____
_____
_____
_____

December 2

_____
_____
_____
_____
_____
_____
_____
_____
_____

December 3

December 4

December 5

December 6

December 7

_____
_____
_____
_____
_____

December 8

_____
_____
_____
_____
_____

December 9

_____
_____
_____
_____
_____

December 10

_____
_____
_____
_____
_____

December 11

_____
_____
_____
_____
_____
_____
_____
_____
_____

December 12

_____
_____
_____
_____
_____
_____
_____
_____

"Too many of us stay walled because we
are afraid of being hurt. We are afraid
to care too much, for fear that the
other person does not care at all."

Eleanor Roosevelt

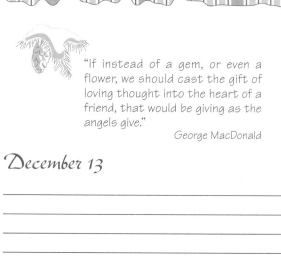

"If instead of a gem, or even a
flower, we should cast the gift of
loving thought into the heart of a
friend, that would be giving as the
angels give."

George MacDonald

December 13

December 14

December 15

_____
_____
_____
_____

December 16

_____
_____
_____
_____

December 17

_____
_____
_____
_____

December 18

_____
_____
_____
_____

December 19

_____
_____
_____
_____
_____

December 20

_____
_____
_____
_____
_____

December 21   First Day of Winter

_____
_____
_____
_____
_____

December 22

_____
_____
_____
_____
_____

December 23

December 24

"A hug is a great gift—one size fits all,
and it's easy to exchange."

unknown

"The best Christmas gift of all is the presence of a happy family all wrapped up with one another."

unknown

December 25

_____
_____
_____
_____
_____
_____

December 26

_____
_____
_____
_____
_____
_____

December 27

_____
_____
_____
_____
_____
_____
_____

December 28

_____
_____
_____
_____
_____

December 29

_____
_____
_____
_____
_____

December 30

_____
_____
_____
_____
_____

December 31

_____
_____
_____
_____
_____

"Now this is not the end.
It is not even
the beginning of the end.
But it is perhaps,
the end of the beginning."

Sir Winston Churchill